KITCHEN
COMMUNION

Cornelia M. Renfroe

John Knox Press
RICHMOND, VIRGINIA

Seventh printing 1973
International Standard Book Number: 0-8042-2400-5

Library of Congress Catalog Card Number: 59-11220
© C. D. Deans 1959
Printed in the United States of America

 KITCHEN COMMUNION

TO
MY MOTHER

KITCHEN

COMMUNION

Kitchen Communion

Time: 7:30 A.M.
Place: Any Woman's Home
Character: *YOU!*

Oh . . . nuts! Seven-thirty already! I can't.
I just can't face it today.
Breakfast,
> dishes,
>> beds,
>>> laundry,
>>>> kids,
>>>>> dirt.

My head aches and I just know that pain
Bob has is another ulcer. He can't stand another operation, and we couldn't pay for it

if he could, and if his folks come this week end I'll die.

Junior! Stop that yowling. I'm cooking as hard as I can. No, Bob, I don't know where a stamp is. For goodness sake! Shall I take my head out of the laundry basket and find one for you? . . . Is that the phone ringing at this hour? If it's Gussie Gossip, tell her I've gone to Alaska. No, no—don't either. She'd believe it and tell it all over town. . . .

Well, hello. Oh, Sue. No, I'm sorry, I can't teach a Sunday school class. Sorry, I haven't the time. No. I told you it was no use to ask me again . . . Well, we may make it to church Sunday, but I doubt it . . . Bob! I'm sorry it hurts, but you brought it on yourself. If you'd just quit stewing . . . Eeeeeek. It's boiling over! Turn the flame down QUICK . . . 'Scuse me, Sue. Family crisis. . . .

Can you read me something? Right now? When I'm . . . when everything is . . . Oh, go ahead. I don't mean to be rude. This is just one of those times. It *is* early. If you weren't such a good friend, I'd hang up. I wish I could get as much out of something as you do that church of yours. . . .

Well, goodness, when will I find time to read the Bible? Do you think reading will help the baby's tooth and Bob's ulcer and that mountain of laundry? . . . Wait till I get my coffee cup . . . Now, shoot! . . . John 15:5-11? Yes, yes, I promise—I will read it . . . Oh, no! Not a poem. Not right now . . . Well, bring it over in 30 minutes. Everyone will be gone by then. 'Bye.

SCRIPTURE

"I am the vine, you are the branches. He who abides in me, and I in him, he it is that bears much fruit, for apart from me you can do nothing. If a man does not abide in me, he is cast forth as a branch and withers; and the branches are gathered, thrown into the fire and burned. If you abide in me, and my words abide in you, ask whatever you will, and it shall be done for you. By this my Father is glorified, that you bear much fruit, and so prove to be my disciples. As the Father has loved me, so have I loved you; *abide in my love*. If you keep my commandments, you will abide in my love, just as I have kept my Father's commandments and abide in his love. These things I have spoken to you, that my joy may be in you, and that your joy may be full."

(JOHN 15:5-11)

Oh, hello, Sue. I guess I'm glad you came. Yes. I just finished reading that Scripture passage you asked me to read. Beautiful words, but they don't mean much in my case. What's your poem? . . . About God's presence through the day? You say it goes with that Bible verse?

I met God in the morning
    When my day was at its best,
And His Presence came like sunrise,
    Like a glory in my breast.

All day long the Presence lingered,
    All day long He stayed with me,
And we sailed in perfect calmness
    O'er a very troubled sea.

Other ships were blown and battered,
    Other ships were sore distressed,
But the winds that seemed to drive them
    Brought to us a peace and rest.

Then I thought of other mornings,
    With a keen remorse of mind,
When I too had loosed the moorings,
    With the Presence left behind.

So I think I know the secret,
    Learned from many a troubled way:
You must seek Him in the morning
    If you want Him through the day!

                (Ralph S. Cushman)

Why, Sue, that's beautiful, and it does fit in with John 15:5-11. That He abide in me . . . and I in Him . . . in love, that His joy be in me—and my joy be full.

Junior, NO. You may *not* take uncooked oatmeal to school to eat at recess and please, put your right shoe on the right foot and not on the left. Thaa-at's right. Which foot does the other one go on? Ooooh Genesis, Exodus, Leviticus, Numbers—Give me patience—Deuteronomy, Joshua, Judges. Kiss me good-bye, darling, and be a good boy. Study hard! . . .

Bless his heart . . . You know, I feel better for some reason. . . .

No, Sue. I don't think the Bible verses and the poem helped *that fast*. Even aspirin with buffering won't do that . . . That poem came out of your booklet there? What is that booklet? . . . Hmmmmm. The ladies in your circle each contributed some Bible verse, prayer, or meditation that had helped them over the rough spots, and you collected them and made a booklet? If I thought anything like that would help me I'd memorize it and recite it all day. It would sound better than my yapping all the time about my troubles. Well, really . . . Oh, never mind. Have some more coffee. You're leaving the booklet? Yes, Sue, I really will read it. I've been peeking anyway . . . 'Bye.

I do feel better. But I wish I *knew* I could abide in His love. Let's see what's next in here. I might as well get some more coffee, read it and find out.

"The Lord will command his lovingkindness in the daytime, and in the night his song shall be with me, and my prayer unto the God of my life."

(PSALM 42:8, K.J.V.)

MEDITATION

It is good to believe that God is with us day and night, sharing every experience. Jesus taught that God is always within human reach, but that we must reach out to Him.

We can begin the day with God by thinking of Him first; of all the good and wonderful things He means to us, depending on Him for complete guidance and help through the day.

At the end of the day, having thought of Him often and talked with Him, we are able to appreciate all He has done for us and to give Him complete thanks.

The best way to begin tomorrow with God is to end today with Him.

Well, now. I hadn't thought about beginning the day thinking of God. Look at the mess of things on my mind this morning. Thinking of one thing or person is certainly less confusing. I guess I didn't exactly mean that. Does Sue mean I can actually *talk* to God? I wish I could, just as I would to a friend. I s'pose you have to use all that language like "causeth" and "maketh" and "thee" and "thy," and I couldn't just talk if I had to say all those words. I wouldn't be me . . . Wait a minute. Here's a prayer that says it about like I would, only a little better . . . that is, if I could pray.

PRAYER

O Lord our God, even at this moment as we come blundering into Thy presence in prayer, we are haunted by memories of duties unperformed, promptings disobeyed, and beckonings ignored.

Opportunities to be kind knocked on the door of our hearts and went weeping away.

We are ashamed, O Lord, and tired of failure. ["I sure am."]

If Thou art drawing close to us now, come nearer still, till selfishness is burned out within us and our wills lose their weakness in union with Thine own. Amen.

(Peter Marshall)

Oh, here's another prayer. Now, how did that man know to say the things I would like to say? The lady who contributed this prayer for the booklet must have felt the same way. This one really hits you. It sure is the truth.

PRAYER

Forgive us, Lord Jesus, for doing the things that make us uncomfortable and guilty when we pray. . . . We are too Christian really to enjoy sinning and too fond of sinning really to enjoy Christianity. Most of us know perfectly well what we ought to do; our trouble is that we do not want to do it. Thy help is our only hope. Make us want to do what is right, and give us the ability to do it. . . . Amen.

(Peter Marshall)

He is right. I don't want to be mean and hateful and selfish, but I don't especially want to give up all my Sundays for church instead of . . . I s'pose one reason I don't pray is that I am ashamed to, but "God helps those who help themselves," you know. Still, I don't seem to be doing so well on my own, Lord knows! Do you know about it, God? Do you?

Is this little thing a meditation? It sure is a clever observation, anyway.

OBSERVATION

Church members in too many cases are like deep sea divers, encased in the suits designed for many fathoms deep, marching bravely to pull out plugs in bath tubs.
(Peter Marshall)

There now, they sure are, and I'm glad to see someone say so for a change. Pious people. Never have any fun. If it's fun, it's a sin. Long face. Don't do this! Don't do that! Wait a minute. Sue isn't like that. She has fun. She doesn't think that because she told that snob, Mrs. Blfspk, to drop dead, that her little Frankie died the very next month, just as punishment for what she said. She didn't mean it anyway. She likes everybody in her church and they play together and they sure *do* work together . . . Heavens to Betsy. If I even pulled out a plug in a bathtub, I bet the water wouldn't run out. Do you s'pose teaching that Sunday school class would be pulling out a little bitty plug? Would it, God? I'm not good enough, you know. But I wish you would show me what to do about teaching, and, God, I sure would need some ability. I sure would!

Here's somebody's favorite Bible verse:

BIBLE VERSE

"I can do all things in him who strengthens me."   (PHILIPPIANS 4:13)

Oh, my—oh, my. If that verse didn't exactly answer what I was just talking about . . . I sure did talk. I s'pose I *was* talking to God. I didn't realize I was. Is *that* the way to do it? Why, that was easy. I really meant what I said, God.

Here it is 10:30 already and I've done no dishes, no laundry. Ugh. Look at that mess of sticky, eggy plates! And at least 15 pairs of dirty jeans. Guess we are better off than I thought. Didn't know we had so many . . . One more peep at that book. *I want a dishwasher.* It says here a Christian housewife is better than a nun. Oh, now, let's not go off the deep end about this. Say something I can believe. Let's see what it says in that Bible reference.

"A good wife who can find?
    She is far more precious than jewels.
The heart of her husband trusts in her,
    and he will have no lack of gain.
She does him good, and not harm,
    all the days of her life.
She seeks wool and flax,
    and works with willing hands.
She is like the ships of the merchant,
    she brings her food from afar.
She rises while it is yet night
    and provides food for her household
    and tasks for her maidens.
She considers a field and buys it;
    with the fruit of her hands she plants
      a vineyard.
She girds her loins with strength
    and makes her arms strong.
She perceives that her merchandise
    is profitable.
    Her lamp does not go out at night.
She puts her hands to the distaff,
    and her hands hold the spindle.
She opens her hand to the poor,
    and reaches out her hands to the needy.

. . . .
She opens her mouth with wisdom,
   and the teaching of kindness is on her
     tongue.
She looks well to the ways of her household,
   and does not eat the bread of idleness.
Her children rise up and call her blessed;
   her husband also, and he praises her:
"Many women have done excellently,
   but you surpass them all."
Charm is deceitful, and beauty is vain,
   but a woman who fears the Lord
     is to be praised.
Give her of the fruit of her hands,
   and let her works praise her in the gates."
(PROVERBS 31:10-31)

No woman could be that good. I don't have very lofty ambitions, but I do wish I wouldn't leave the dishes, and would have things done on time, and have more sympathy for Bob. I do, I really have sympathy for him, God. I do. I'm just scared. I yell at him so he won't know how scared I am. When he suffers so I wish I could hurt for him . . . "Her children rise up and call her blessed; her husband also." Well, God, I'm not going to say what my husband called me the other day, and I hope you didn't hear it. Now why did I say that? I guess you know why he said it. He had no clean socks and I burned that nice sirloin steak that he went all the way to the market for, and "I Love Lucy" was on. Well, yes, it was late, but the kids had eaten cookies and bananas . . . No, God, Bob didn't eat cookies and bananas all afternoon and he was hungry. I got nervous because I was late and didn't do him any good and he called me that You-Know-What. But he didn't mean it. At least I don't think so. He was upset. But I don't really think he meant it . . . That woman in the Bible opened her hands to the poor and needy. Well . . . Didn't I give a lot of Junior's old jeans and T shirts? They were too small for him and some were out at the knees a little. I cut the buttons off that coat but it was still pretty good. If the folks who get it are smart enough, they'll sew some more on. I gave the things to the Salvation Army, God. I didn't have any room for them and . . . Oh, me, God. How selfish can you get! I sure didn't get the plug out of the tub on that one, did I? I hadn't realized how mean and stingy I was. I'll just never make the grade with that woman in Proverbs as my goal. But God, I'll try. Help me try, and help me to stick to it. Thanks . . . Let's see, what's next. No wonder Sue liked this booklet. . . .

MEDITATION AND PRAYER

A Christian Housewife is more Holy than a Nun. . .
                              (Martin Luther)

There is a legend that an angel once came to Anba Piterius, a holy man of Egypt, and told him that in a nearby convent he might find a truly holy woman. All the nuns passed before him, but none was the one he sought. "Is there no other?", he asked. "No, none at all," said the Mother Superior. "Except, of course, the maid. But she is only a drudge, the broom of the whole place." But when the holy man saw her, he fell upon his knees before her. "We are creatures of no account," he said, "but this woman is your mother and mine. I entreat God that He will give me a portion with her on the day of judgment."

"A Christian housewife is more holy than a nun because she does more good in the world," declared Martin Luther. "Washing dishes, cleaning house, tending babies, can in themselves be a high calling from God."

PRAYER: We thank Thee, Father, for making us housewives and mothers. May we ever be proud of our jobs, and may we realize the tremendous opportunity we have to teach your will to everyone in our household and to create a truly happy and Christlike atmosphere in our homes which may be an inspiration to all in an insecure world. Amen.

Warm all my kitchen with Thy love
And fill it with Thy peace;
Forgive me all my worrying
And make all grumbling cease.

Thou who didst give men food
In room and by the sea,
Accept this service that I do;
I do it unto Thee.

(By an English servant girl.)

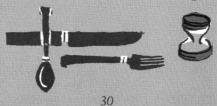

I just don't know how I feel about all that.
Maybe if I get up from here and wash the
dishes, I can figure it out. At least my con-
science will feel better. I just noticed something. My headache's gone and I don't know
when it left. In fact, I didn't even miss it.
Nasty, icky dishes. I hate 'em. I certainly
couldn't dedicate a sinkful of old dishes to
You. I'm sure You would want them clean.
But, God, don't you understand why I hate
them so? I hope somebody does.

Every time I mention a dishwasher to the
girls, the hateful old buzzards . . . oops, I
mean the mean old things look down their
noses at me and say, Why, a few little dishes.
Nothing to it. I can do them while I'm making
a dress, baking a cake, and preparing Jamaica
Duck for dinner. The sauce is very tricky.
What! You don't have your dishes done? My
work is done by nine o'clock. She meant A.M.
too—not P.M. like me. God, I'm going to copy

that prayer I just read and put it here in the kitchen. I can see being a mother and dedicating a child to You. I can see reason in creating a Christian home and making it a haven for your family and a sanctuary in your Name (which I haven't done any of, but will try to do so much better). But God, I have to grow in this business. You see, I had spoken to You sometimes, but I didn't think You bothered. Why should You? What had I done for You? I still haven't done anything. But I know that I can't solve my troubles by myself. They really aren't so bad—except Bob's illness. But today, I found out You listened and You care. I can "abide" in You!

But, God, I can't ask You to accept my dishwashing service, not yet. I have to grow some more. I still hate them. But I hope I don't grumble so much. Knowing I can talk out what's bothering me with You helps. I probably won't stop right away. I know me.

Oh, dear! I tried to turn a page in Sue's book and read while I washed these old—I mean these dishes. I got the pages wet. But see what is on them. It's funny, I know. I needed this. It's coincidence; it's also Sue. She just ignored how mean I was. She had something and she shared with me. I see what it is now and what her church does and why they love it. It says so right there. From the Bible, too. You don't have to turn to the back for the answers, either. They are all through it. How many things have I looked up the answer to today? If I didn't find out exactly what I was looking for I found what I thought was a pretty good substitute. By that time I could see that the substitute or compromise wouldn't do and I saw the answers. Just listen to this:

33

SCRIPTURE

"Love is very patient, very kind.
 Love knows no jealousy;
 love makes no parade,
 gives itself no airs,
 is never rude,
 never selfish,
 never irritated,
 never resentful."
(I CORINTHIANS 13:4-5, Moffatt)

"In nothing be anxious; but in everything by prayer and supplication with thanksgiving let your requests be made known unto God."
(PHILIPPIANS 4:6, A.S.V.)

"Ask, and it shall be given you; seek, and ye shall find; knock, and it shall be opened unto you: For every one that asketh receiveth; and he that seeketh findeth; and to him that knocketh it shall be opened."
(MATTHEW 7:7-8, K.J.V.)

Those are the answers, all right, to most of my problems. But have I goofed! That business about love being patient and kind, not jealous or rude—and, God, not selfish. My family has been all of these things to me and I accepted it all and thought I had an awfully hard time. I did, too, in the state of mind I had been so downright mean as to let myself get in. "Love is never irritated." Bob must love me, and You, too, God. I didn't mean to leave You out. Bob sure couldn't have put up with all that foolishness if he hadn't. The only time he was irritated (at least where it showed) was when he called me a—well, I told You that, You know. I just took everything and didn't give anything and didn't understand. When You made us, did You ever think we'd be such awful nincompoops? You did a wonderful job and we just messed it up.

This thing about Thermostats or Thermometers and which one are you? Well, let's see. It's almost the end of the book. They talk about the funniest things in this book. You just never know what women will think of next . . . or why, either.

Thermostats or Thermometers

A thermometer . . . hangs on the wall in a place so that it can be easily seen by the occupants of the room and the temperature ascertained. It hangs alone. It has no power to make the room hot or cold. It reflects its environment and adjusts itself to it. A thermostat looks much like a thermometer. It also hangs on the wall, but it has powerful connections. If it is hot, it has ways of making it cooler. If it is cold, it has means by which to make it warm. Instead of being affected by its environment, it changes its environment. A thermostat does something about its surroundings while a thermometer adjusts itself to its environment.

There is a vast difference. People can be classified into thermometers and thermostats. Thermometer personalities are chameleons, adjusters, compromisers. They always take on the color, climate, morality, and spirituality of the group they are with. They merely reflect their environment. They do nothing to change it. Thermostat personalities are changers, reformers, leaders, transformers. They are not satisfied with the *status quo*. Things must improve. So, something begins to happen—they have connections. They do their human part, but they also send an impulse—a prayer to God—to the powerhouse above. . . "We need help. Things must be different. The moral and spiritual climate must change. It's too cold and frigid and freezing. We must have power, fire, heat, to burn and change our world, our nation, and our churches." Thermostats get things done. Thermometers surrender to conditions.

(Source unknown.)

38

Well, how funny . . . I mean the comparison. Now was I a thermostat gone haywire or a thermometer just stuck on freezing and staying that way so long that people were fooled into thinking that was the only kind of weather they would ever get . . . namely, my poor froze-up husband and children. I'll think about it and try to figure it out the next time I wash dishes. Yep, that's what I said. *Wash 'em.* This is a do-it-yourself project. No dishwasher for me . . . But do I have to look forward to it?

● ● ●

Do you mean it's one o'clock? Where went lunch? Don't guess I had any. As usual, all I've done is wash the dishes and drink about a gallon of coffee. You see how it is, don't You? I got up with so many good intentions. I meant to . . . wait a minute. I read a booklet. Just a few pages in it, but it changed my perspective. I see I don't love enough, don't give enough, don't pray enough, and don't believe

39

enough. I don't see much to put down on the credit side, except I want to do those things. I want my home to be the haven in the book— my children to grow in the knowledge of You. But God, it's an awful big job. Your know my background. It's a mess. You expect such an awful lot from people. And You go right on listening just as if you expect me to be that new person, to reach that goal. Well, it's too high, God. I can't reach it alone. I want to, but I'll get scared. After all, You made me. I can't help being this way! No, no. I didn't mean that. I'm sorry. You made me all right. But I ruined your property myself. I'll try to fix it. But please, God, show me what it was You wanted and help me. I can't do it by myself.

Gracious sakes, girl! What's the matter with you? You get right over there and look at the last page in Sue's book. It worked all day, didn't it? Well, go on! Look!

BIBLE VERSE

"Bear ye one another's burdens, and so fulfil the law of Christ." (GALATIANS 6:2, K.J.V.)

LEGEND: *"Bear Ye One Another's Burdens"*

There is an old legend which tells us that long ago the birds had no wings. They were content to walk about eating and singing, but never flying.

Finally, the Lord called on the animals, each to carry a burden. But each refused.

One of the birds decided to try, and with great difficulty assumed the burden and stumbled along with the weight on its back. Gradually, the load became lighter and it began to lift the bird off the ground. The other birds soon followed, and before long all the birds were flying. The burdens had become wings!

Christ can turn our burdens into wings that will lift us up to realms of joy and service, and by bearing our burdens and the burdens of others, we may so fulfill the law of Christ.

Well, that was my answer. I knew You wouldn't let me down. Bear my burdens in love and You'll give me wings. How good You have been to me! Why couldn't Sue have come sooner? I'm sorry. I could have found You. Some people don't use all the sense You gave 'em, God. After You have been so good to give me these little bitty wings, God . . . They are just little nubbins, really. But I feel some of the load lifted and I have only just come barely into the room. When I do more for you, and learn more, they'll grow. I'd sorta like blue feathers, God. Do You mind? Now tell me something I can do for You. I want to do something to show You I am grateful. I'll teach that class, but honestly, I feel sorry for them. Maybe if I'm a nicer person Bob won't stew and worry so much and that old ulcer will dry up of pure starvation, or maybe if it doesn't we'll think of something to do about it together. You and Bob and me.

42

I'm still so pitifully, awfully human, but You know that anyway, so maybe You won't mind if I add this. And I'll sure be here tomorrow. I bet we really get things done. That is . . . I'll do them, God. Just please let me know You are there.

But . . . I still don't like to wash dishes.

POEM

God—there are things in my life I don't like,
  Folks I can't bear;
But there are more things I would hate to change,
  Friends I can't spare.
So when you hear me complaining aloud,
  Just turn away;
Deep inside my ungracious heart, I am
  Grateful each day.
                    Amen.
          (Margueritte Harmon Bro)

QUOTED MATERIAL
(In order of appearance)

"I am the vine, you are the branches." . . . John
15:5-11. Unless otherwise indicated, Scripture quo-
tations are from the Revised Standard Version,
copyright 1946 and 1952 by the Division of Christian Education of the National Council of the
Churches of Christ in the United States of America.

"I met God in the morning" . . . "The Secret,"
from *Spiritual Hilltops,* copyright 1932 by Ralph S.
Cushman. By permission of Abingdon Press.

"The Lord will command his lovingkindness" . . .
Psalm 42:8, King James Version.

"It is good to believe that God is with us" . . .
Adapted from a meditation by Richard L. Ownbey
in *Strength for Service to God and Country,*
edited by Norman E. Nygaard and Arthur S.
Ward. Nashville: Abingdon Press, 1950. Used
by permission.

"O Lord our God, even at this moment" . . .
from *Mr. Jones, Meet the Master,* edited by Cath-
erine Marshall, p. 47. Westwood, N. J.: Fleming
H. Revell Company, 1949. Used by permission.

"Forgive us, Lord Jesus" . . . *ibid.,* pp. 129, 145.

"Church members in too many cases" . . . *ibid.,* p. 34.

"I can do all things" . . . Philippians 4:13.

"A good wife who can find?" . . . Proverbs 31:10-31.

The section "Meditation and Prayer" was prepared by Dr. and Mrs. William M. Ramsay, and is reprinted from *Presbyterian Women,* May, 1957. Used by permission.

"A Christian Housewife is more Holy than a Nun" . . . Adapted from statements by Martin Luther concerning the Christian wife and mother.

"There is a legend" . . . Adapted from *Through Lands of the Bible,* by H. V. Morton, p. 228. New York: Dodd, Mead & Company, 1938. Used by permission.

"Warm all my kitchen with Thy love" . . . Attributed to an English servant girl.

"Love is very patient, very kind." . . . I Corinthians 13:4-5, Moffatt translation, arranged.

"In nothing be anxious" . . . Philippians 4:6, American Standard Version.

"Ask, and it shall be given you" . . . Matthew 7:7-8, King James Version.

"A thermometer . . . hangs on the wall" . . . Source unknown.

"Bear ye one another's burdens" . . . Galatians 6:2, King James Version.

"There is an old legend" . . . Adapted from *Streams in the Desert* by Mrs. Chas. E. Cowman, p. 202. Los Angeles: Cowman Publications, 1925. Used by permission.

"God—there are things in my life" . . . From *Every Day a Prayer,* by Margueritte Harmon Bro, p. 316. New York: Harper & Brothers, 1943. Used by permission.